Rating Observation Scale for Inspiring Environments

Jessica DeViney, Sandra Duncan, Sara Harris, Mary Ann Rody, Lois Mitten Rosenberry

"This book is dedicated to the children and staff of Children's Discovery Center who constantly inspire us to keep our environments blooming."

(c) 2010 Jessica DeViney, Sandra Duncan, Mary Ann Rody, Sara Harris, Lois Rosenberry

Published by Gryphon House, Inc.

PO Box 10, Lewisville, NC 27023

800.638.0928 (toll free); 877.638.7576 (fax)

Graphic Designers: Jessica DeViney, Patrick DeViney

Visit us on the web at www.gryphonhouse.com

Reprinted November 2020

Bulk purchase

Gryphon House books are available for special premiums and sales promotions as well as for fund-raising use. Special editions or book excerpts also can be created to specification. For details, contact the Director of Marketing at Gryphon House.

Disclaimer

Gryphon House, Inc. and the authors cannot be held responsible for damage, mishap, or injury incurred during the use of or because of activities in this book. Appropriate and reasonable caution and adult supervision of children involved in activities and corresponding to the age and capability of each child involved is recommended at all times. Do not leave children unattended at any time. Observe safety and caution at all times.

Rating Observation Scale for Inspiring Environments

A COMPANION OBSERVATION GUIDE FOR *INSPIRING SPACES FOR YOUNG CHILDREN*

jessica deviney

sandra duncan

sara harris

mary ann rody

lois rosenberry

Lewisville, NC

introduction

The *Rating Observation Scale for Inspiring Environments* (ROSIE) is designed to evaluate environments of young children. ROSIE encourages you to evaluate your classroom from a new perspective by considering and observing aesthetic design elements such as color, focal points, texture, lighting, displays, and the use of space and nature.

SPROUTING, BUDDING, AND BLOOMING

Designed as an educational tool, ROSIE provides specific indicators to identify the first level of growth, which is Sprouting. ROSIE helps you learn what to do to reach the Budding stage and, ultimately, grow to the highest level of aesthetic beauty, known as Blooming.

SPROUTING

In the SPROUTING STAGE, a plant begins to peek through the dirt and shoots appear. During this stage, you are beginning to understand the principles of designing aesthetically beautiful spaces. Although your environment has started the growing process, time and nourishment are needed to develop into flower buds.

BUDDING

In the BUDDING STAGE of growth, a plant begins to stand tall and prepare to blossom. During this stage, you are becoming more competent at creating inspiring spaces. As your knowledge increases about design principles and aesthetic components, your environment continues to develop into a cluster of buds.

BLOOMING

The BLOOMING STAGE is the period of time when a plant is at its highest level of growth and it glows with health and beauty. It is during this stage that you have reached your fullest potential in designing beautiful and inspiring spaces for children and adults.

seven principles of design

ROSIE'S companion book, *Inspiring Spaces for Young Children,* and the ROSIE offer Seven Principles of Design that will help you make your classroom Bloom.

principle 1: nature inspires beauty   page 11

Just as you are immersed in a natural world of sights, sounds, tastes, smells, and textures, classrooms should reflect the wonders of nature that surround you. As children interact with nature, they deepen their understanding and appreciation of their roles as caretakers of the planet.

principle 2: color generates interest   page 15

Color can be a powerful design principle both in positive and negative ways. Proper use of color can create a mood, define a space, and reflect children's homes and communities. On the other hand, color can be overpowering, confusing, and over-stimulating. A neutral background with a few well-chosen accent colors will create interest that is focused on the children and adults who inhabit the space.

principle 3: furnishings define space   page 19

Furnishings identify classroom areas such as dramatic play, blocks, art, music, and science. When these furnishings are authentic and properly sized and placed, children's play will increase in quality and depth.

principle 4: texture adds depth   page 29

Texture in the environment offers visual interest and depth and provides children with unusual tactile experiences. As children interact with sensory items, they sharpen their observational skills and fine motor abilities through the languages of weaving, sculptures, and textiles.

principle 5:   displays enhance environment   page 31

By eliminating clutter, arranging storage materials, and highlighting children's work, the classroom becomes a backdrop to honor all who occupy the space.

principle 6:   elements heighten ambiance   page 41

Multiple sources of light create an ambiance of relaxation and contemplation. By using multiple sources of light in supportive ways, children are able to interact creatively with others and the environment.

principle 7:   focal points attract attention   page 45

When entering the classroom, a distinct focal point can highlight interactive learning centers, chldren's work, an architectural element, or a beautiful artifact. Focal points invite children to actively engage in the environment.

INSPIRING SPACES FOR YOUNG CHILDREN

ROSIE'S accompanying book, *Inspiring Spaces for Young Children*, gives you ideas, inspirations, and projects that can be completed in a few minutes, a few hours, or on a weekend. The book gives you a step-by-step process for designing an aesthetically pleasing classroom. Although some ideas are moderately priced, most cost just a few dollars.

Examining children's spaces through aesthetic lenses will inspire you to go beyond the high standards of quality rating scales and accreditation. *Inspiring Spaces for Young Children* and ROSIE encourage you to create places of beauty that nurture children, families, and staff. *Inspiring Spaces for Young Children* is available through Gryphon House, Inc. For more information on the *Inspiring Spaces for Young Children*, visit gryphonhouse.com.

determining your ROSIE level

As you prepare to determine your ROSIE level of growth, the first step is to become an objective observer who looks at the classroom from an aesthetic perspective.

getting started

- The ROSIE Observation Scoring Guide determines your level of growth in creating an aesthetically beautiful environment.

- There are three levels of growth: 1) Sprouting, 2) Budding, and 3) Blooming. These levels must be identified for each of the Seven Principles of Design (pages 2-3).

- Each of the Seven Principles of Design has several indicators, which are specific to the principle. The number of indicators varies from principle to principle. You determine your highest level of growth (either Sprouting, Budding, or Blooming) for every indicator in each principle.

- The observation takes at least two hours to complete. It is preferable to conduct the observation when children are not present. Although it is not mandatory to conduct the entire observation in a single block of time, it is important to finish within a week.

calculating your ROSIE level

To calculate your level, follow the ROSIE Observation Scoring Guide example (page 5) using these steps:

1. Begin with Principle 1: Nature Inspires Beauty (page 7).

2. Read across the three levels (Sprouting, Budding, and Blooming) of Indicator #1 to determine which level best reflects your classroom environment. For example, in Principle 1/Indicator 1, you must have at least one living item in your classroom to reach the Sprouting level valued at one point. No points are earned if your classroom does not have something living. *Note: Underlined words in each principle are defined on page 44.*

3. Your goal is to reach the next highest level of growth. You receive one point for Sprouting, two points for Budding, and three points for Blooming.

4. Once you have determined your level of growth, circle the one number that completely reflects your level on the ROSIE Observation Scoring Guide. Because the ROSIE book is designed for repetitive use, simply make a copy of the blank Scoring Guide on page 47.

scoring example

5. On the ROSIE Observation Scoring Guide, calculate your subtotal score for Principle #1 by adding together all of your indicator points. Record this subtotal at the bottom of the column of Principle #1. This subtotal will determine if you are in the Sprouting, Budding, or Blooming level for this principle.

6. Continue your observation and calculate a subtotal score for each of the seven principles.

7. Each principle's subtotals added together will determine your overall level of growth: Sprouting is 1-73 points; Budding is 74-124 points; and Blooming is 125-147 points.

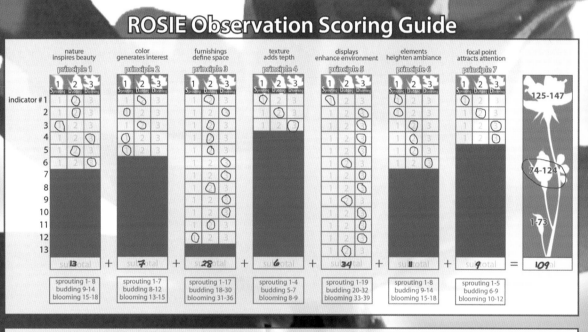

Helpful Hints

*   Be patient. Do not be discouraged if your initial score falls within the sprouting or budding stages. Growth takes time.

*   Make an action plan. Improve your score by implementing the next level's indicators into your classroom.

*   Start small. Focus on one indicator at a time.

*   Change what you can. Know that some ROSIE indicators may be outside your ability to improve.

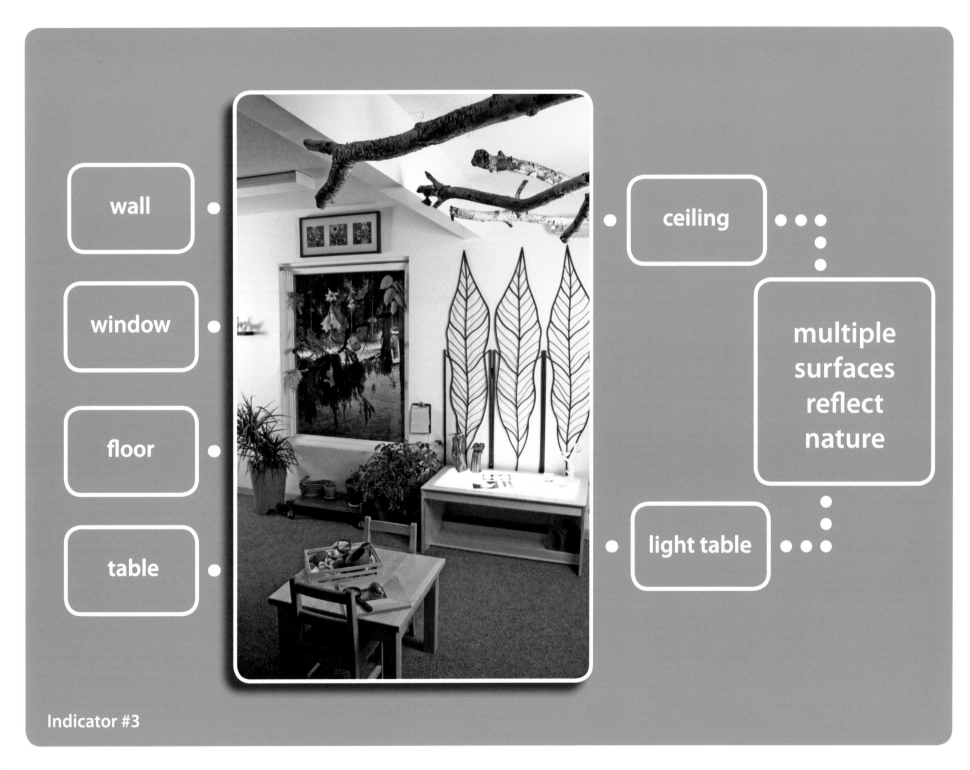

wall

window

floor

table

ceiling

multiple surfaces reflect nature

light table

principle 1: nature inspires beauty

indicator #1

1	2	3
There is one living item in the classroom.	There are two different types of living items in the classroom.	There are three or more different types of living items in the classroom.
Examples: plant, small animal, fresh flower, fish, water wall or fountain		

indicator #2

1	2	3
There is evidence of items from nature being used in a SENSORIAL experience (e.g., twigs and leaves in the sensory table).	There is evidence of items from nature being used in a sensorial experience AND a CREATIVE experience (e.g., painting with twigs).	There is evidence of items from nature being used in a sensorial, creative, AND COGNITIVE experience (e.g., arranging twigs according to length).

indicator #3

1	2	3
There is one item from nature displayed on one surface.	There are two items from nature displayed on two surfaces.	There are three or more items from nature displayed on at least three surfaces.
Examples: ceiling, shelf, counter, table, wall, window, floor		
Examples: hanging shell curtain, sea grass rug, photograph of nature		

sprouting   budding   blooming

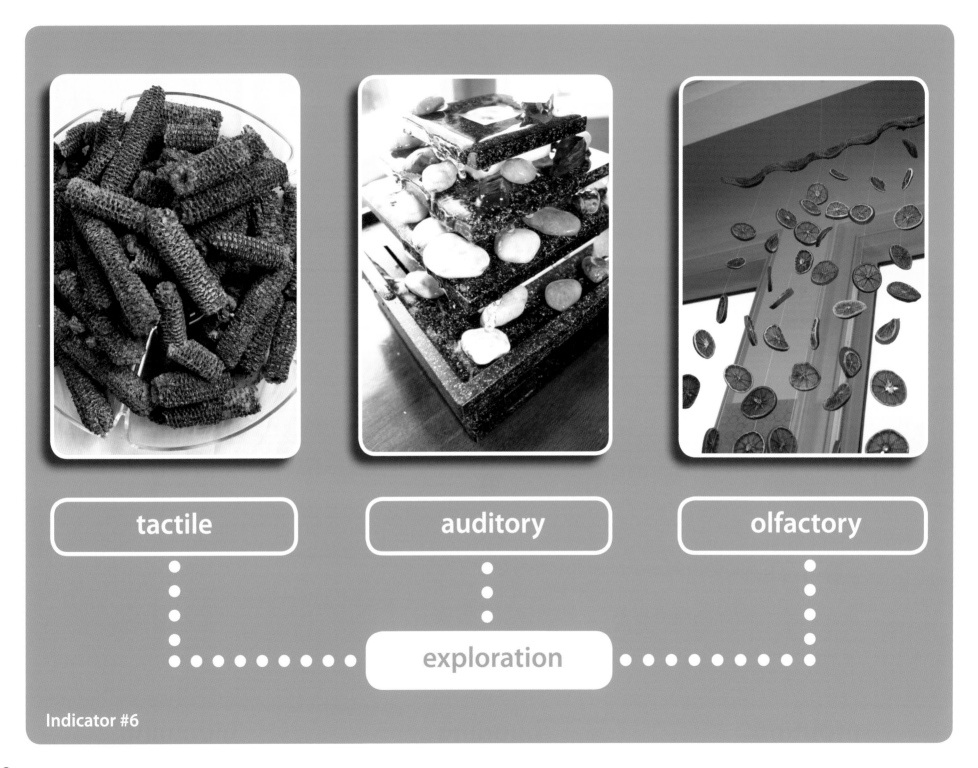

tactile

auditory

olfactory

exploration

Indicator #6

principle 1: nature inspires beauty

	1	2	3
indicator #4	There is one example of <u>children's work</u> inspired by nature. Examples: clay sculpture of a bird, framed observational drawing of tree, weaving made of natural materials	There are two examples of children's work inspired by nature.	There are three or more examples of children's work inspired by nature.
indicator #5	There is one example of nature used in a practical way. Examples: rocks as book ends, tree stump as chair, wooden bowl as container, tree branch as curtain rod, log as balance beam, tree pieces as blocks	There are two examples of nature used in a practical way.	There are three or more examples of nature used in a practical way.
indicator #6	One nature item is accessible to children that encourages <u>TACTILE</u> exploration. Examples: molding clay, sorting seashells, sifting sand, corn cobs	One nature item is accessible to children that encourages tactile exploration AND a different nature item that encourages <u>AUDITORY</u> exploration. Examples: listening to rain stick, conch shell, table water fountain	One nature item is accessible to children that encourages tactile exploration, another nature item that encourages auditory exploration, AND a different nature item that encourages <u>OLFACTORY</u> exploration. Examples: smelling fresh flowers, pine branches, herbs, dried fruit

sprouting   budding   blooming

accent colors generate interest

principle 2: color generates interest

indicator #1

1

Furniture is a mixture of colors and wood tones.

Examples: tables, shelves, storage units, housekeeping sets

2

With the exception of upholstered furniture, there are no more than three furniture colors in the entire room.

3

With the exception of upholstered furniture, most furniture is wood-toned and/or neutral colors.

indicator #2

1

While many colors and patterns of <u>décor elements</u> are outdated, there is evidence of current <u>color trends</u> being introduced.

Examples: wall paper border, curtain, rug

2

Most décor elements reflect current color trends.

3

All décor elements reflect current color trends.

indicator #3

1

Some surfaces are <u>primary colors</u> while at least two different types of surfaces are <u>neutral colors</u>.

Examples: wall, countertop, trim, carpet, ceiling, hard floor

2

Few surfaces are primary colors while at least three different types of surfaces are neutral colors.

3

Neutral colors are used on at least four different types of surfaces and other colors are only used as <u>accent colors</u>.

sprouting   budding   blooming

décor element inspires accent colors

inspiration

principle 2: color generates interest

1

Accent colors are inspired by a décor element.

Examples: rug, curtain, pillow, upholstered chair, art piece

2

Accent colors are inspired by a décor element AND limited to no more than three colors.

3

Accent colors are inspired by a décor element, limited to no more than three colors, AND the accent colors are repeated throughout the room.

1

Accent colors are integrated into the classroom through paint and/or fabric.

2

Accent colors are integrated into the classroom through paint and/or fabric AND natural materials.

Examples: potted greenery, painted tree branch, bamboo wall divider

3

Accent colors are integrated into the classroom through paint and/or fabric, natural materials, AND unconventional or <u>authentic</u> objects.

Examples: child-painted tiles, wall-mounted scarf

sprouting   budding   blooming

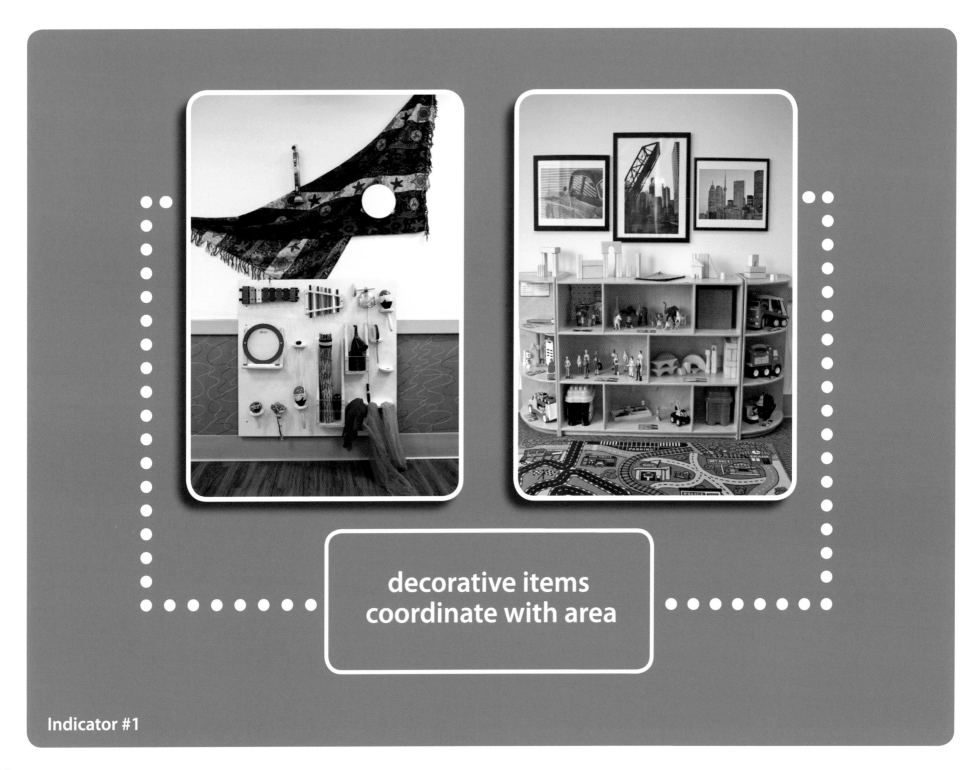

decorative items coordinate with area

Indicator #1

principle 3: furnishings define space

	1	2	3
indicator #1	Each of two learning centers must have its own coordinating decorative item. Examples: cityscape photograph in block area, hanging instruments in music area	Each of three learning centers must have its own coordinating decorative item.	Each of three learning centers must have its own coordinating decorative item, AND one item is child created.
indicator #2	There is a designated <u>private space</u> where a child can be alone.	There is a designated private space where a child can be alone, AND it includes at least two soft elements. Examples: pillows, upholstered chair, rug	There is a designated private space where a child can be alone that includes at least three soft elements, AND its own source of light Examples: window, flashlight, lamp
indicator #3	There are designated spaces within the classroom for staff supplies and personal items.	There are designated AND concealed storage spaces within the classroom for staff supplies and personal items.	The staff USES designated and concealed spaces for storing supplies and personal items.

sprouting   budding   blooming

authenticity enriches environment

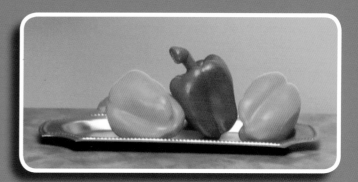

Indicator #4

principle 3: furnishings define space

indicator #4

1

Most classroom furniture and equipment have been purchased from an early childhood supplier.

2

At least two small , authentic items have been added to each learning center.

Examples: tool belt, place mats, teapot, telephone, road maps, dental x-rays

3

At least two small, authentic items are in each learning center, AND a large authentic furniture piece has been added to the classroom.

Examples: wooden dresser, painted armoire, upholstered chair, small buffet, hanging lamp

indicator #5

1

The furniture pieces are in proportion to each other (e.g., chairs are the right size for tables).

2

The furniture pieces are in proportion to each other AND are the right size for the classroom space.

Note: Smaller spaces may require combination equipment such as a one-piece kitchen set.

3

The furniture pieces are in proportion to each other, are the right size for the classroom space, AND are balanced by similarly sized furnishings (e.g., rug fits within the learning center).

indicator #6

1

Learning centers are defined in typical ways (i.e., shelves are placed at perpendicular angles or flush with wall).

2

Some learning centers are defined by positioning furniture parallel to each other to create a unique angle (e.g., 45 degrees) with the rest of the room.

3

Learning centers are defined by positioning furniture AND rugs at unique angles with the rest of the room.

sprouting   budding   blooming

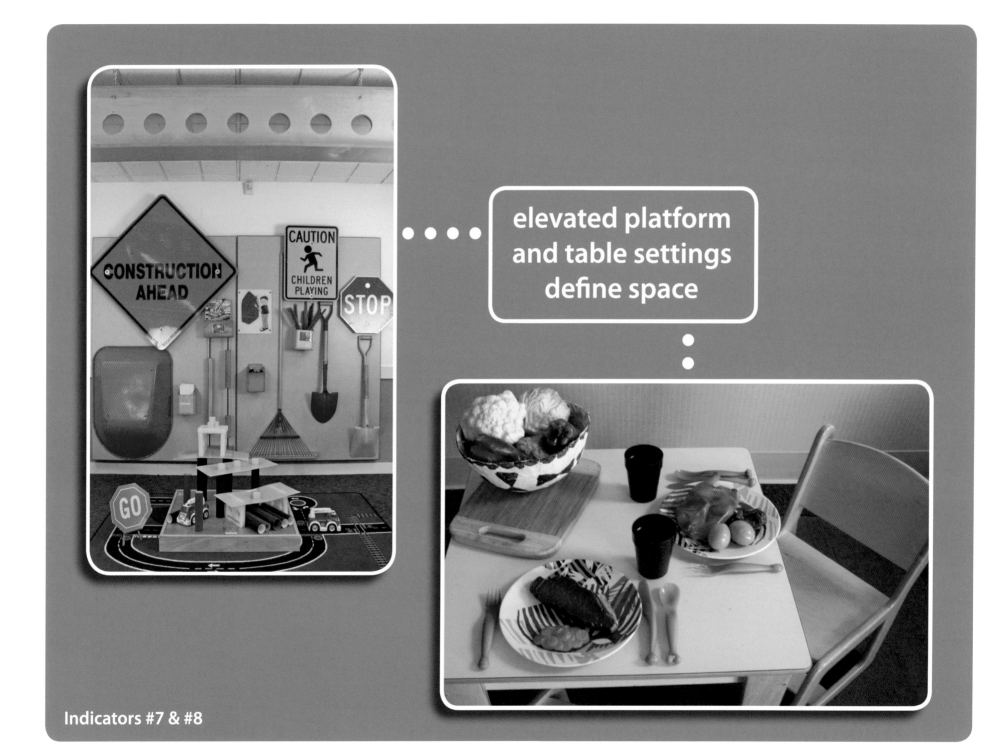

elevated platform and table settings define space

Indicators #7 & #8

principle 3: furnishings define space

indicator #7

1

The children's home living center's table is set with dishes, silverware, place mats, and cups.

2

The children's home living center's table is set AND dolls are clothed.

3

The children's home living center's table is set, all dolls are clothed, AND there are authentic materials in the dramatic play area.

Examples: pot holders, baking utensils, cookbooks

indicator #8

1

There is a designated area for building (e.g., elevated platform, rug).

2

There is a designated area for building AND authentic items have been added.

Examples: measuring tape, road signs, working gloves

3

There is a designated area for building, authentic items have been added, AND children have personalized the area by creating their own cars, buildings, and/or neighborhoods with various materials.

Examples: cardboard tubes, maps, blocks, grid blocks, log building sets

sprouting   **budding**   **blooming**

professional artist tools

● ● ● ● ● authentic elements enhance learning centers ● ● ● ● ●

natural materials

Indicators #9 & #10

principle 3: furnishings define space

1
There is a designated art area for children to create artwork on at least two surfaces.

Examples: tables, easel, projector, light table, wall-hung boards such as dry erase or chalkboards

2
There is a designated art area for children to create OR view artwork on three or more surfaces.

3
There is a designated art area for children to create or view artwork on three or more surfaces, AND these surfaces include authentic items.

Examples: artist paintbrushes, art palette, smock, professional art books

1
There is a designated science area for children to explore.

2
There is a designated science area for children to explore natural materials and use science equipment.

Examples: scale, microscope, magnets, magnifying glasses

3
There is a designated science area for children to explore natural materials, and use science equipment, AND an organized system to test theories and record their findings.

sprouting   budding   blooming

furnishings reflect learning areas

Indicators #11 & #12

principle 3: furnishings define space

indicator #11

1

There is a designated music area where instruments are displayed and available for children's use.

2

There is a designated music area where instruments are displayed and available for children's use AND it includes multicultural instruments.

Examples: Mexican maracas, African drum

3

There is a designated music area where instruments are displayed and available for children's use, and it includes multicultural instruments, AND a recording device for use by children.

Examples: karaoke player, digital recorders, CD player

indicator #12

1

A quiet reading area has been positioned away from walking paths.

2

A quiet reading area has been positioned away from walking paths, AND at least two authentic elements have been added.

Examples: coffee table, rug, hanging/table light, basket, pillows, blanket

3

A quiet reading area has been positioned away from walking paths, AND at least three authentic elements have been added.

sprouting   budding   blooming

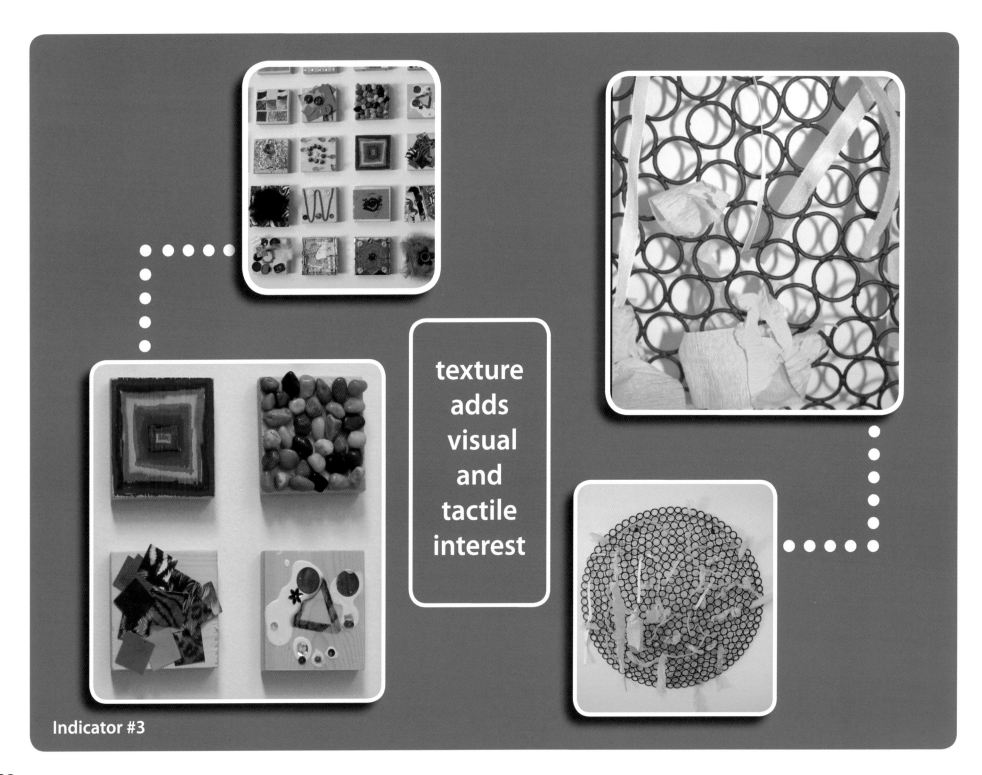

texture adds visual and tactile interest

principle 4: texture adds depth

	1	2	3
indicator #1	Two types of flooring are used to add texture. Examples: carpet, rugs, tile, hardwood, brick	Two types of flooring are used to add texture, AND it corresponds to the area it occupies. Examples: synthetic fall surface in gross motor, washable tile in art area, soft rug in reading area	The texture of two types of flooring corresponds to the area it occupies AND there is one type of flooring that exhibits or reflects nature. Examples: sea grass rug, wood decking, pebble mat
indicator #2	Conventional items are used to create visual interest through texture. Examples: throw pillows, upholstered furniture, hanging fabrics	Conventional AND natural items are used to create visual interest through texture. Examples: woven baskets, textile tablecloths, wooden bowls	Conventional, natural, AND unconventional items are used to create visual interest through texture. Examples: hanging glass globes, shutters, lattice, privacy screens, or a birdcage
indicator #3	The children's work adds texture through use of textiles (e.g., decorated fabric squares).	The children's work adds texture through the use of textiles AND through weaving. Examples: jute, scarves, corn husks, ribbon, natural fibers	The children's work adds texture through textiles, weaving, AND sculpture. Examples: wire, boxes, clay, stones, recycled materials

sprouting   **budding**   **blooming**

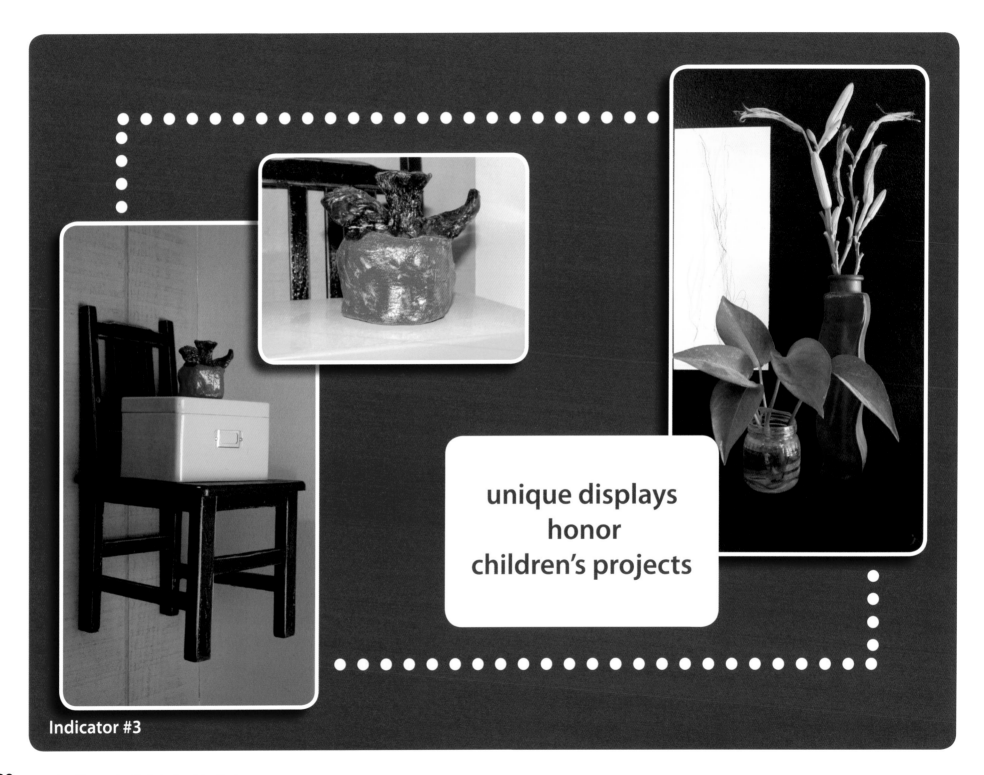

unique displays
honor
children's projects

Indicator #3

principle 5: displays enhance environment

indicator #1

1

Four or more commercially prepared teaching materials are displayed.

Examples: calendar, alphabet, and helper chart

2

No more than three commercially prepared materials are displayed.

3

No commercially prepared materials are displayed.

indicator #2

1

Supporting elements of displays have some color and pattern.

Examples: borders, frames, bulletin board background

2

Supporting elements of displays have minimal color and pattern.

3

Supporting elements of displays are neutral and do not have pattern.

indicator #3

1

Child-made displays and projects have been created in a typical way with common materials.

Examples: crayons, markers, fingerpaint

2

Child-made displays and projects have been created using artistic materials.

Examples: clay, wire, natural materials, tiles, beads

3

Child-made displays and projects have been created using artistic materials AND are displayed in unexpected ways or with the authentic inspiration.

Examples: clay letters displayed in shadow box; wire sculpture in a flowerpot; art displayed on hanging chair

sprouting   budding   blooming

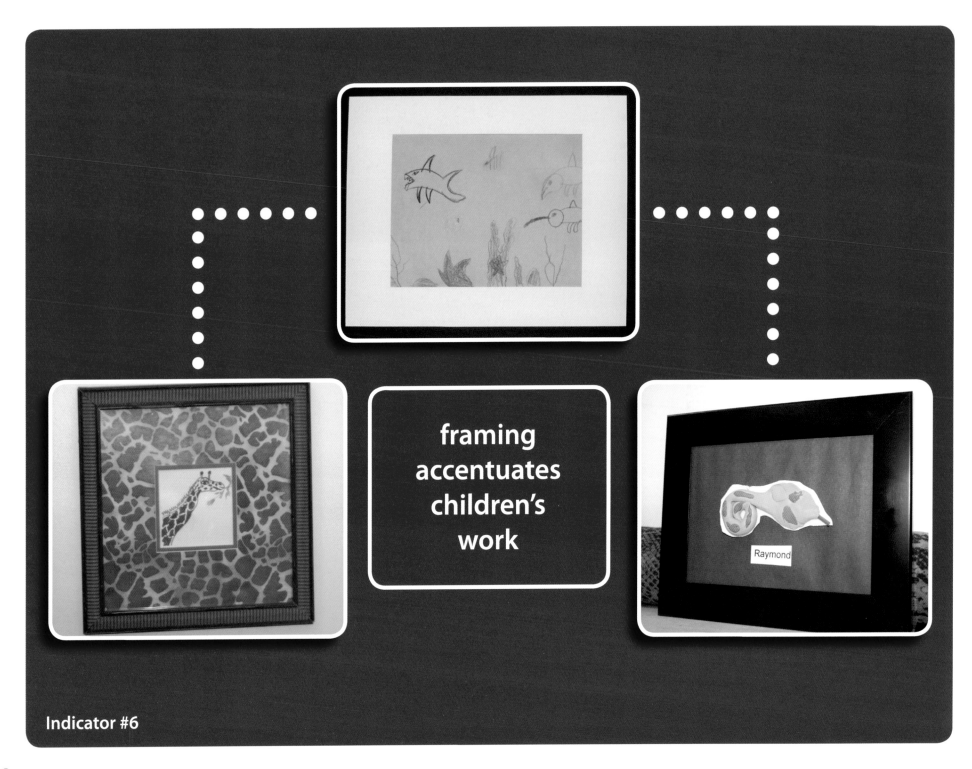

framing accentuates children's work

Raymond

principle 5: displays enhance environment

	1	2	3
indicator #4	Displays of children's work reflect current learning experiences.	Children's current work is attractively arranged in a designated area that provides white space between displays.	Children's current work is grouped together based on content, is displayed in a related learning center or designated area, AND provides white space between displays.
indicator #5	Signage is grammatically correct.	Signage is grammatically correct AND uses appropriate uppercase and lowercase letters.	Signage is grammatically correct, uses appropriate uppercase and lowercase letters, AND is die-cut, computer generated or authentically made by children.
indicator #6	The mounted display of children's work has straight edges.	Neatly trimmed children's work has been purposefully mounted on background material.	Most children's work is framed with edges hidden by frame, matting, or mounting.

sprouting   budding   blooming

shelf

ceiling

• • • • • • surfaces of display • • • • • •

Indicator #9

principle 5: displays enhance environment

indicator #7

1	2	3
Wall displays are framed with construction paper, tag board, or other paper-type materials.	Some wall displays are in commercially purchased frames.	Most wall displays are in commercially purchased frames AND are appropriately grouped together according to topic, style, or subject.

indicator #8

1	2	3
Half of the furnishings and cabinet doors are free of paper clutter.	All furnishings and cabinet doors are free of paper clutter.	All furnishings and cabinet doors are free of paper clutter AND required paperwork is displayed on magnet, bulletin, cork, or wall boards located in designated areas.

indicator #9

1	2	3
Displays are limited to one surface. Examples: wall, floor, shelf, ceiling, window, mirror	Displays are visible on two surfaces.	Displays are visible on at least four surfaces.

sprouting   budding   blooming

scissors in brick

magnifying glasses
in grass

paint brushes
in popcorn

• • •   **stored materials
raised to an artform**   • • •

Indicator #10

principle 5: displays enhance environment

indicator #10

	1	2	3

1

Supplies and materials are displayed and stored in typical containers.

Examples: plastic baskets, transparent bins

2

Some supplies and materials are displayed and stored in typical containers, AND half are displayed and stored in unique ways.

Examples: crayons in standing silverware holder, paper in hanging shoe pockets

3

Some supplies and materials are displayed and stored in typical containers, half are displayed and stored in unique ways, AND two are raised to an art form.

Examples: scissors displayed in brick, paintbrushes in clear bowl of popcorn kernels

indicator #11

1

Children's framed artwork is visible in the classroom.

2

Children's framed artwork is visible in the classroom AND placed at children's eye level.

3

Children's framed artwork is visible in the classroom with some examples placed at children's eye level, AND others at adults' eye level.

sprouting   budding   blooming

organized materials

Sensory Balls

Pinecones

Magnets

principle 5: displays enhance environment

indicator #12

1	2	3
Various colored containers are used throughout the classroom (e.g., green for pencils, red for paper, yellow for chalk).	Containers are the same color and used throughout the classroom (e.g., only green containers are used throughout the classroom).	Neutral-colored bins, natural baskets, and/or transparent containers are used throughout the classroom.

indicator #13

1	2	3
Objects and containers on each shelf categorically belong together (e.g., puzzles and blocks are on separate shelves).	Categorically organized objects are placed on shelves in an uncluttered way, with space between each object.	Categorically organized objects are placed on shelves in an uncluttered way with a space between each object AND there is a system that children use to retrieve and replace objects. (e.g., pictures/drawings and/or names of items on the shelf).

sprouting   budding   blooming

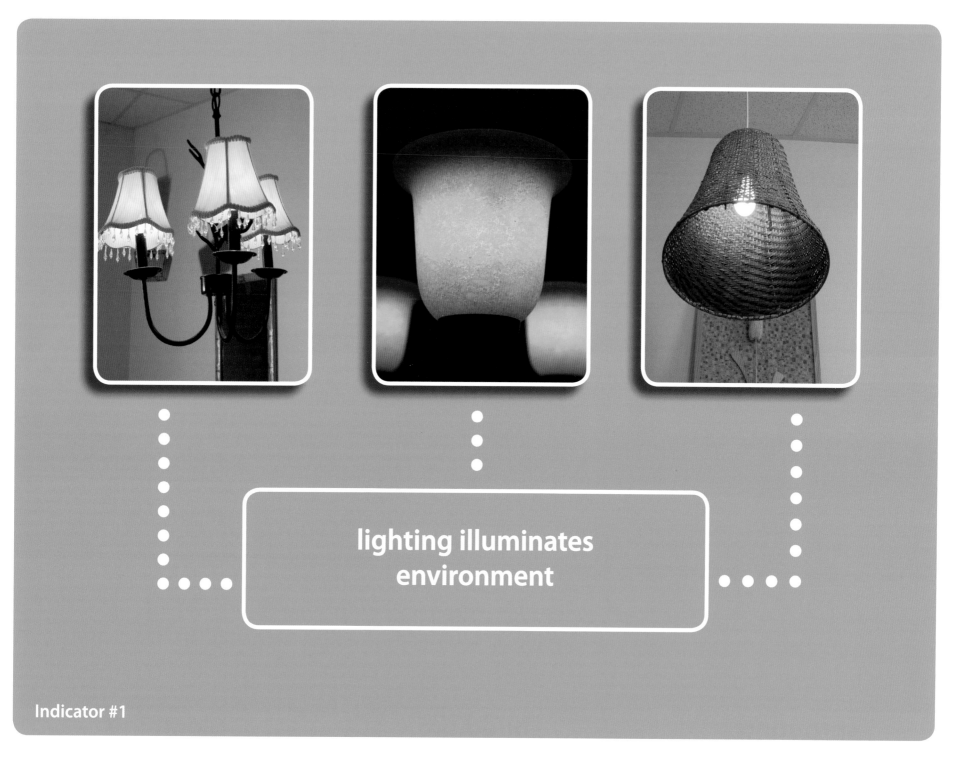

lighting illuminates environment

principle 6: elements heighten ambiance

1
Only permanent light sources are used in the classroom, such as windows and ceiling lights.

2
Sources of light not only come from permanent sources, but also from table and floor lamps, hanging light fixtures or lanterns, filtered/diffused light, and spotlights.

3
Sources of light are used intentionally to create various ambiances, lighten a dark space, and/or spotlight areas or objects of interest.

1
Lighting is only used to provide illumination.

2
One creative use of lighting is evident in the classroom.

Creative Lighting Examples: light boxes, shadow screens, light tables, lanterns, light ropes, garden lights, light focused on artwork

3
Several creative uses of lighting are evident in the classroom.

1
There is one source of lighting and this light source can only be off or on.

2
There are several sources of lighting, but these sources can only be off or on.

3
There are several sources of lighting, and at least one source can be dimmed for different times of the day.

sprouting

budding

blooming

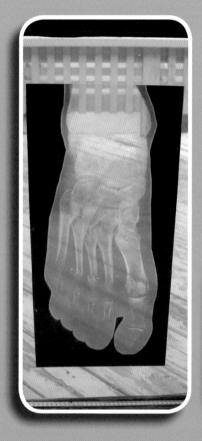

transparency and light enhance objects

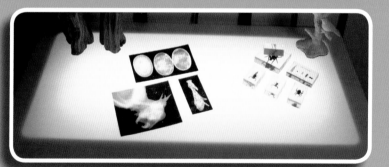

Indicators #4 & #6

principle 6: elements heighten ambiance

	1	2	3
indicator #4	Shadow play elements are available for children. Examples: overhead project, flashlights, shadow box, spotlight, screen	Shadow play elements are available AND used by children to create light and shadow experiences.	Shadow play elements are available, used by children, AND intentionally support learning experiences with additional props. Examples: blocks, costumes, puppets
indicator #5	All sounds are used intentionally by coordinating with activities. Examples: classical music for naptime, upbeat rythmic songs for gross motor and movement activities	Sounds are used intentionally AND are multicultural. Examples: African drum, Mexican maracas	Sounds are used intentionally, are multicultural, AND include sounds of nature. Examples: rainstick, fountain, sound machine
indicator #6	Objects on windows are transparent.	Objects on windows are transparent AND items placed on windowsills do not block the light.	Objects on windows are transparent, items placed on windowsills do not block the light, AND light is used as an educational tool. Examples: viewing crystals, x-rays, or prisms, looking through kaleidoscope, measuring shadows

sprouting   budding   blooming

textural elements enhance focal points

principle 7: focal points attract attention

	1	2	3
indicator #1	The first area evident upon entering the classroom is a children's learning center and not a custodial space. Examples: diaper changing area, cubbies, restroom, cots	The first area evident upon entering the classroom is a learning center with most of the shelving units forward-facing.	The first area evident upon entering the classroom is a learning center with ALL shelving units forward-facing or perpendicular to the entry.
indicator #2	An interactive <u>focal point</u> geared towards children is evident upon entering the classroom. Examples: recipe book, cutting board	An interactive focal point geared towards children is evident upon entering the classroom AND enhanced in at least two ways. Examples: curtain divider, rug, artwork	An interactive focal point geared towards children is evident upon entering the classroom, enhanced in at least two ways, AND incorporates a unique element (e.g., buffet in the home-living center).
indicator #3	There is evidence of a focal point but other elements distract from it (e.g., visual clutter, too much or too little visual stimulation).	There is some evidence of a focal point AND there are some empty spaces on the walls to avoid visual over-stimulation.	There is an intentional focal point that is clearly defined and there is a balance of empty and filled spaces on the walls.
indicator #4	Focal points have been enhanced by a visual element. Examples: mural, accent color	Focal points have been enhanced by a visual element AND a textural element. Examples: tapestry, fabric, netting	Focal points have been enhanced by visual elements, several textural elements, AND authentic pieces. Examples: lantern, sleeping bag, compass

sprouting	budding	blooming

DEFINITIONS

Accent Colors are used sparingly to emphasize or highlight another color in a décor element.

Auditory describes what is experienced though hearing.

Authentic refers to an object that is commonly seen in an adult space but is placed in the children's environment for an aesthetic purpose or to enhance functionality.

Children's Work encompasses the writings, drawings, paintings, and sculptures that the child produced.

Cognitive involves the process of thinking, knowing, or perceiving.

Color Trends reflect color combinations that are popular at a specific point in time. By utilizing current color trends, the space is kept fresh and up-to-date.

Focal Point is what first draws the attention of the viewer upon entering the classroom.

Neutrals do not appear on the color wheel; they include white, gray, black, brown, and beige.

Olfactory describes what is experienced through the sense of smell.

Primary Colors are red, blue, and yellow and cannot be made from any other color.

Private Space is an area that only 1 or 2 children can occupy at a time and may be separated by a transparent wall, curtain panel, or loft level.

Sensorial refers to aspects of the environment that stimulate the physical senses of sound, touch, taste, smell, and sight.

Tactile refers to the various textural elements that produce a sensation when viewed or touched (e.g., rough, smooth, hard, soft).

ROSIE Observation Scoring Guide

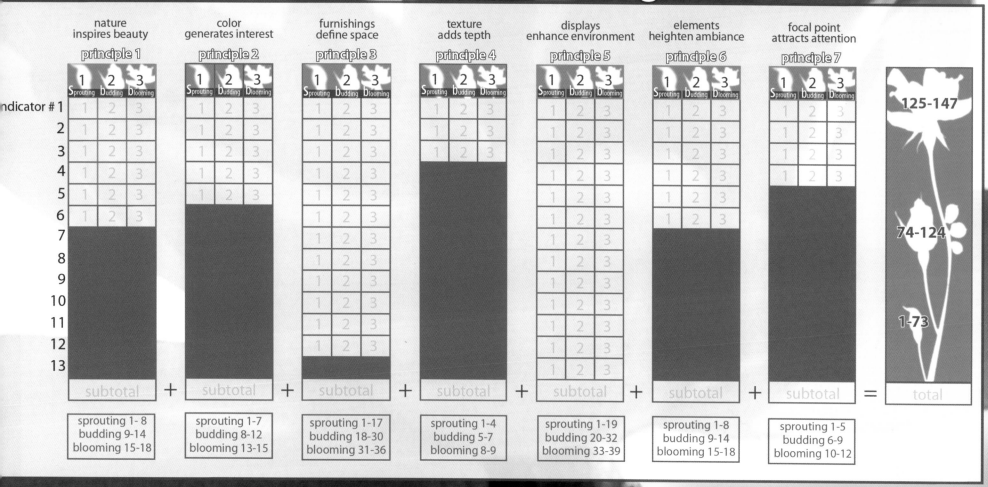

	principle 1 nature inspires beauty			principle 2 color generates interest			principle 3 furnishings define space			principle 4 texture adds tepth			principle 5 displays enhance environment			principle 6 elements heighten ambiance			principle 7 focal point attracts attention		
	1 Sprouting	2 Budding	3 Blooming	1 Sprouting	2 Budding	3 Blooming	1 Sprouting	2 Budding	3 Blooming	1 Sprouting	2 Budding	3 Blooming	1 Sprouting	2 Budding	3 Blooming	1 Sprouting	2 Budding	3 Blooming	1 Sprouting	2 Budding	3 Blooming
indicator # 1	1	2	3	1	2	3	1	2	3	1	2	3	1	2	3	1	2	3	1	2	3
2	1	2	3	1	2	3	1	2	3	1	2	3	1	2	3	1	2	3	1	2	3
3	1	2	3	1	2	3	1	2	3	1	2	3	1	2	3	1	2	3	1	2	3
4	1	2	3	1	2	3	1	2	3				1	2	3	1	2	3	1	2	3
5	1	2	3	1	2	3	1	2	3				1	2	3	1	2	3			
6	1	2	3				1	2	3				1	2	3	1	2	3			
7							1	2	3				1	2	3						
8							1	2	3				1	2	3						
9							1	2	3				1	2	3						
10							1	2	3				1	2	3						
11							1	2	3				1	2	3						
12							1	2	3				1	2	3						
13							1	2	3				1	2	3						
	subtotal			+ subtotal			+ subtotal			+ subtotal			+ subtotal			+ subtotal			+ subtotal			= total

125-147

74-124

1-73

sprouting 1- 8 budding 9-14 blooming 15-18	sprouting 1-7 budding 8-12 blooming 13-15	sprouting 1-17 budding 18-30 blooming 31-36	sprouting 1-4 budding 5-7 blooming 8-9	sprouting 1-19 budding 20-32 blooming 33-39	sprouting 1-8 budding 9-14 blooming 15-18	sprouting 1-5 budding 6-9 blooming 10-12

classroom:	principles of excellence:
observer:	principles for improvement:
date of observation:	action plan:

2